LOOK IT UP
Now in a fully revised edition

1. You and Your Body
2. People and Customs
3. What People Do
4. The Prehistoric World
5. Ships and Boats
6. People of Long Ago
7. The Sea
8. The Earth
9. Cold-Blooded Animals
10. Warm-Blooded Animals
11. Sport and Entertainment
12. The World of Machines
13. Land Travel
14. Flying
15. Outer Space
16. Index

Photo Credits: Airbus Industrie; Anglia TV; Ardea; Peter J. Bish; Austin J. Brown; Philip Clark; Bruce Coleman; Graham Finch; Imperial War Museum; Matt Irvine; BBC Hulton Picture Library; Spectrum Colour Library; ZEFA.

Front cover: Spectrum Colour Library.

Illustrations: Jim Bamber; Robert Burns; Dick Eastland; Philip Emms; Colin Hawkins; Ron Haywood; Eric Jewell; Vanessa Luff; Wilfred Plowman; Mike Roffe; George Thompson; Raymond Turvey; Michael Whelply.

First edition © Macmillan Publishers Limited, 1980
Reprinted in 1981, 1982, 1983 and 1984
Second edition © Macmillan Publishers Limited, 1985

All rights reserved. No reproduction, copy or transmission of this publication in any form or by any means, may be made without written permission

Chief Educational Adviser
Lynda Snowdon

Teacher Advisory Panel
Helen Craddock, John Enticknap, Arthur Razzell

Editorial Board
Jan Burgess, Rosemary Canter, Philip M. Clark, Beatrice Phillpotts, Sue Seddon, Philip Steele

Picture Researchers
Caroline Adams, Anne Marie Ehrlich, Gayle Hayter, Ethel Hurwicz, Pat Hodgson, Stella Martin, Frances Middlestorb

Designer
Keith Faulkner

Contributors and consultants
John E. Allen, Neil Ardley, Sue Becklake, Robert Burton, Barry Cox, Jacqueline Dineen, David J. Fletcher, Plantagenet Somerset Fry, Bill Gunston, Robin Kerrod, Mark Lambert, Anne Millard, Kaye Orten, Ian Ridpath, Peter Stephens, Nigel Swann, Aubrey Tulley, Tom Williamson, Thomas Wright

Published by Macmillan Children's Books
a division of Macmillan Publishers Limited
4 Little Essex Street, London WC2R 3LF
Associated companies throughout the world

ISBN 0 333 39732 0 (volume 14)
ISBN 0 333 39568 9 (complete set)

Printed in Hong Kong

Flying

Second Edition
LOOK IT UP

Contents

	Page
FLYING ANIMALS	**4**
How birds fly	6
Flying insects	8
Gliding animals	10
FLYING MACHINES	**12**
Balloons	14
Gliders	16
Airships	18
AEROPLANES	**20**
Early aeroplanes	22
Planes for peace and war	24
The record breakers	26
Seaplanes	28
Famous aircraft	30
Passenger planes	32
Aircraft at war	34

	Page
Supersonic planes	36
Concorde and the Space Shuttle	38
Helicopters	40
Cargo aircraft	42
Small aircraft	44
Special aircraft	46

HOW AIRCRAFT ARE MADE	**48**
Making planes	50
Making the Airbus A300	52

AIRPORTS	**54**
Pilots and crew	56
Airport staff	58
Air traffic control	60
Planes of the future	62

DID YOU KNOW?	**64**
INDEX	

FLYING ANIMALS

Many animals can move through the air but only birds, bats and insects fly properly. They flap their wings to keep themselves in the air. Other animals, such as the flying lizard, only glide. The flying fish wriggles its tail in the water to take off. Some spiders are carried through the air on a silk thread.

How birds fly

Birds are well designed for flying. Their feathers help to lift them and move them in the air. Powerful muscles in the breast work to flap their wings. Different birds have different-shaped wings. Swifts have narrow wings for flying fast. Vultures have broad wings for gliding. Baby birds have to learn to fly.

vultures

hummingbird

Hummingbirds get their name from the noise their wings make. They beat their wings about 80 times a second. Hummingbirds hover near flowers and sip nectar. They are the only birds that can fly backwards.

A bird's wings do two things. They work in the same way as aircraft wings to lift the bird upwards. They also push the bird forwards.

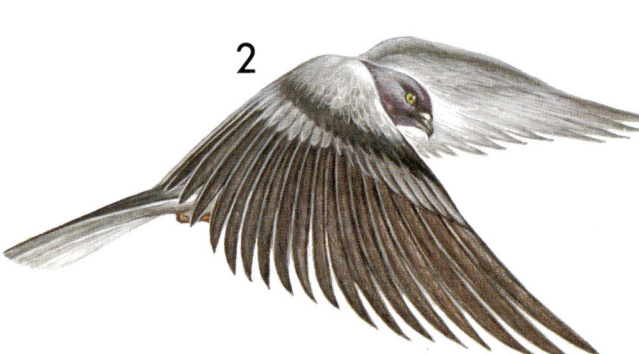

On the downstroke, the wings are spread out. They push down and back. This propels the bird forwards and upwards.

On the upstroke, the bird is freewheeling. The wings are twisted so that the bird is not pushed down and back again.

Flying insects

Most insects have two pairs of wings, which usually beat in time. They beat their wings very fast. Mosquitoes beat their wings more than 500 times a second.

The bumblebee gets its name from the noise made by its wings as they lift its heavy body.

longhorn beetle

bumblebee

Beetles have a front pair of wings with hard, shiny lids. These are not used for flying. They fit over its back and protect the delicate back wings. When the beetle is flying, the hard wings are held out so the back wings can beat freely.

The house-fly has only one pair of wings. Behind the wings is a pair of tiny clubs which help the fly to balance properly.

clubs

Gliding animals

Several kinds of animal can glide long distances. They do not have proper wings. Flying squirrels and flying phalangers have flaps of skin between their legs. The flying frog has large webbed feet and the flying snake flattens its body as it leaps. They all glide down from trees.

FLYING MACHINES

For thousands of years men watched birds fly and wished they could do the same. There are many stories about people long ago who tried to fly. None of them was successful.

Today we still cannot fly like birds. Aircraft can carry us quickly and safely to most parts of the world.

An old Greek story tells how Icarus tried to fly with wings made of wax and feathers. The sun melted the wax and Icarus fell into the sea.

There is a very ancient tale about a British king who thought that he could fly. He was called Bladud. The story says he made himself a pair of wings so that he could fly over London. When he tried them out he could not fly at all. He fell and was killed.

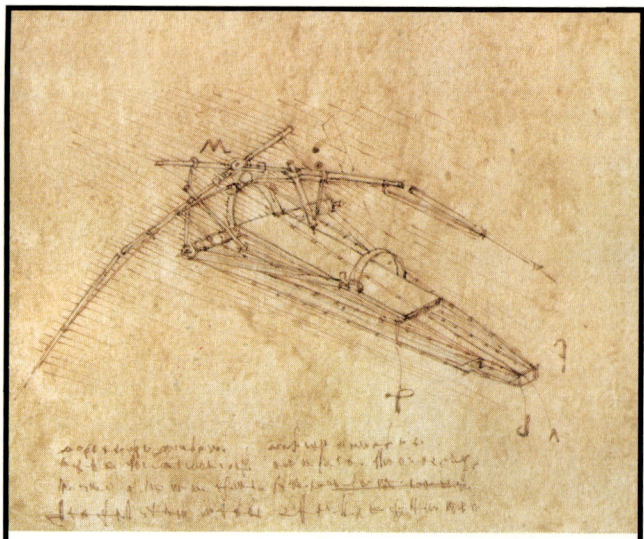

Leonardo da Vinci lived 500 years ago. He was very interested in flying. He made drawings of machines with flapping wings. This was his man-powered aircraft.

Kites were made in China 5,000 years ago. It was not until 1852 that kites big enough to lift up a man were made. In this picture Colonel Cody is being lifted up by a very large kite.

The first flying machines were like kites. They had two sets of wings and were called gliders. They did not have engines. Some were fastened to ropes and towed along by cars or speed boats.

There were no planes with engines 90 years ago. It is amazing how quickly people have learned the secrets of flight. Today aircraft like Concorde, above, can fly faster than a bullet from a gun.

Balloons

Men flew in balloons long before planes were made. A Frenchman called Charles flew a balloon about 200 years ago. It was filled with hydrogen. This is a gas which is lighter than air. It made the balloon rise up and fly. Balloons cannot be steered. They are pushed along by the wind. The balloon on the right is a modern gas balloon.

Nowadays hot air ballooning is a sport. Sometimes balloons like this one are used for advertising.

Two Frenchmen, the Montgolfier brothers, built this hot air balloon They used fire to heat the air inside the balloon. When the air got hot the balloon rose up into the sky. Their first flight was in 1783.

Gliders

A glider is a simple kind of aircraft. It has no engine so it has to be towed into the sky. It is often fastened to a small plane by a strong cable. When the plane takes off it tows the glider behind it.
Up in the air the cable drops away. Then the glider rides up and down on currents of air.

Modern gliding is a wonderful sport. This glider can be taken apart and put on a trailer. Then it can be taken home after a flight. You can see the trailer in the background.

Sir George Cayley made a glider in 1852. It carried one man and had a tailplane and a rudder to steer with. A copy of his glider was built a few years ago. You can see it in the picture above. It was towed along the runway behind a car. It flew very well.

The Wright brothers were the first men to fly successfully. It was on 17 December 1903. First they experimented with gliders. This one looked like a box kite.

17

Airships

An airship is a balloon driven by an engine. The first one was invented by Henri Giffard in 1852. Later airships could carry 50 passengers. Some flew across the Atlantic at speeds of about 100 kilometres an hour. Some airships broke up or caught fire. After these accidents no more giant airships were built.

This airship is fastened to a mast. Passengers went up the mast in a lift to get on board the airship.

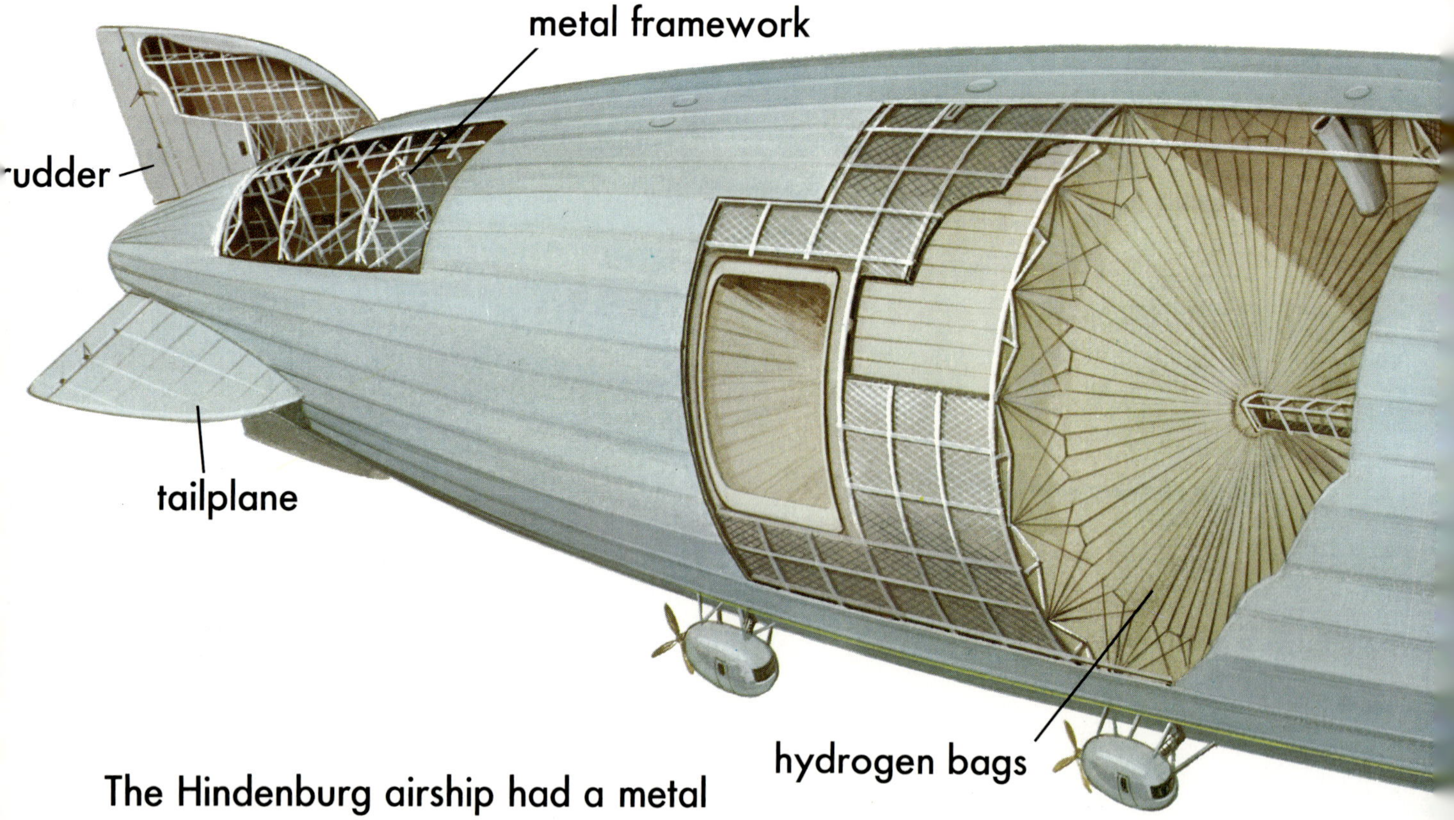

The Hindenburg airship had a metal framework. Hydrogen gas was kept between the frames in large bags. It caught fire in 1937.

blimp

This airship is called a blimp. It does not have a metal framework.
The gas inside gives it its shape.

passenger area

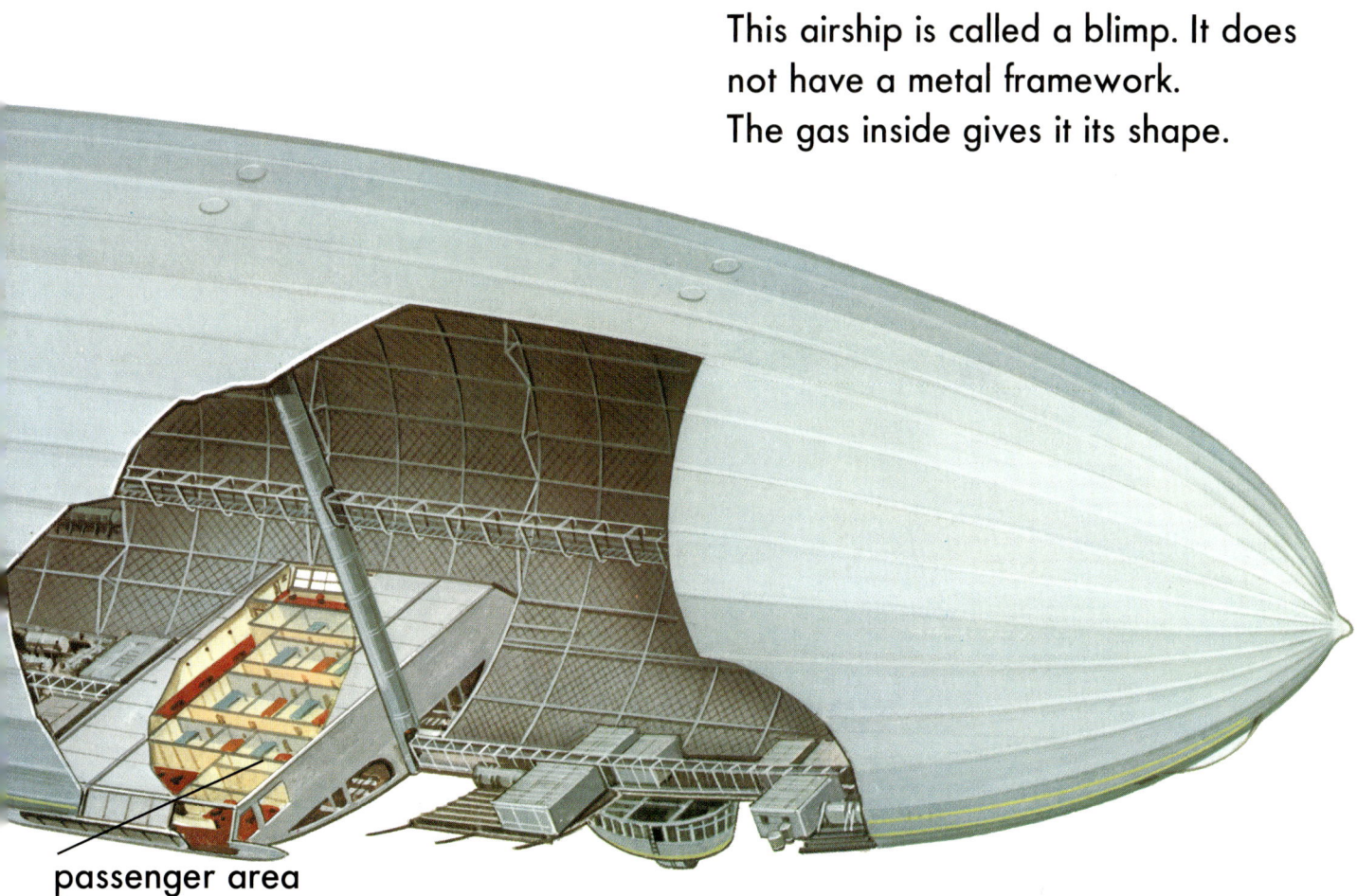

AEROPLANES

Early aircraft

The Wright brothers lived in America. At first they made bicycles. Then they became interested in flying. They built their own gliders. These experiments taught them about flight. They learned how the air moves. They also found out how to make light, strong structures.

The first flight December, 1903

This kite was the first flying machine made by the Wright brothers. Strings were tied to the wings. A man on the ground pulled the strings to keep the wings level.

This glider kite was large enough to carry one man. Wilbur Wright flew in it for just 10 seconds. He found out that aircraft controls have to work very quickly.

The Wright brothers were clever engineers. For four years they designed and experimented. At the end of this short time they built the first plane to fly. They learned how to control it and turn it in the air. They also learned how to land safely. They were the first men to fly properly.

3

In 1903 the Wright brothers flew the first real plane. It had a petrol engine and two propellers. The brothers designed and built every part of it themselves.

4

Soon the Wright brothers could fly for as long as an hour. Now their plane had a seat for a passenger as well as the pilot. It was the world's first passenger aircraft.

Early aeroplanes

In 1908 the Wright brothers took one of their planes to Europe. This encouraged other people to build and fly aircraft. There were many new designs. Not all of them were successful. Soon flying became a popular sport. Great races were held. People went to flying displays to see the aeroplanes.

Blériot

Farman

Farman

Planes for peace and war

Special fighter planes were built in the First World War. They carried guns and could shoot at soldiers on the ground or aircraft in the sky. Later on in the war bombers were made. After the war some firms which had made bombers built the first airliners.

Handley Page airliner

This was one of the first war planes. The propeller was behind the pilot's seat. Another man sat in the front and fired the gun.

Vickers FB5 biplane

This German fighter had three wings and could fly well. The famous German pilot called the Red Baron flew in one of these planes.

Fokker triplane

The record breakers

After the war new planes were built with more powerful engines. Aircraft could fly long distances without stopping to refuel.

Pilots flew to many parts of the world for the first time. Soon airlines were started. They carried passengers to distant countries.

In 1927 Charles Lindbergh flew non-stop from New York to Paris in this plane. It took him 33 hours.

In 1919 Alcock and Brown made the first non-stop crossing of the Atlantic. It took them 16 hours. On the way Brown had to climb out of his seat to knock ice off the plane.

Amy Johnson was a famous British pilot. She flew on her own from England to Australia in 19 days.

In 1931 the first planeload of airmail arrived in England from Australia in this large biplane.

Seaplanes

Seaplanes and flying boats take off and land on water. The large craft in the picture is called a flying boat. Its body rests right in the water. This one was built in 1938 to carry a heavily loaded seaplane into the air.

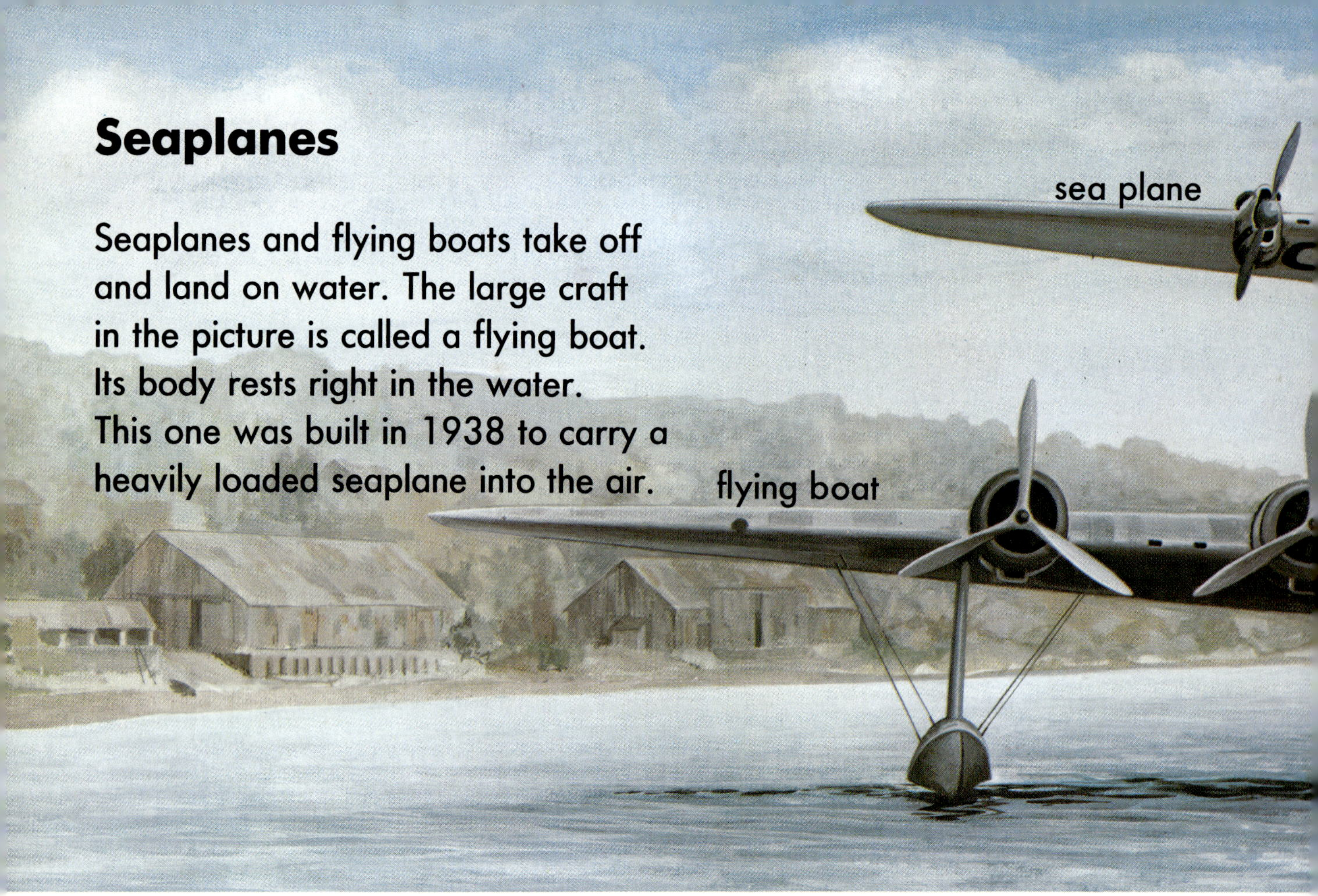

Seaplanes like the one above land on small lakes. People sometimes use them for sport. These planes cannot fly very fast. Their heavy floats slow them down. On the right is a large pasenger flying boat.

28

float

This is a Japanese amphibian plane. It is able to land either on water or a runway. This one is used for rescuing people at sea. It is specially designed to take off and land in rough seas.

29

Famous aircraft

Here are some of the world's most famous aircraft. You can see how much planes have changed. The early biplanes were covered in struts and wires. One-winged planes came next. They are called monoplanes. They flew faster and were stronger. Later jet engines were invented. Jet planes fly very fast.

Louis Blériot flew from France to England in this 1909 monoplane.

This big Russian biplane was built in 1913. It has four engines.

This German monoplane was one of the first metal aircraft.

This airliner carried passengers from England to Africa and India in 1932.

This American plane of 1935 was the first modern airliner.

6

This British flying boat flew to Africa and Australia.

7

This American plane of 1939 was the first large aircraft to fly high.

8

The Comet was the first jet airliner. From 1949 it flew at 800 kph.

9

This Russian airliner was the fastest propeller plane of its day.

10

The American Tri-Star was one of the first 'wide-bodied' aircraft.

11

Concorde is today the only airliner to fly faster than sound.

31

Passenger planes

Nowadays 500 million people travel by jet airliner every year. The Boeing 747 Jumbo Jet is the largest jet airliner. It can carry 550 people. Airliners with propellers are used for shorter trips. The Dash 7 carries 70 passengers. Its engines are specially designed to be very quiet.

Jumbo Jet

Most big passenger planes are made in the USA. The only big one made in Europe is the Airbus. Parts for the plane are made in five European countries. They are sent to a factory in southern France where they are put together. The Airbus can carry 270 people.

Early airliners were slow, noisy, draughty and cold. The bumpy ride often made passengers sick.

Aircraft at war

Many of the planes made today are war planes. Some of them are bombers. Some are fighter planes that can shoot down other aircraft. Other war planes take photographs of enemy countries.

This American F-15 fighter flies at more than twice the speed of sound.

The Tornado is a swing-wing aircraft. It can fly slowly when the wings are spread out. When the wings are folded back it can fly twice as fast as the speed of sound.

Most war planes have ejection seats. The pilot can escape from his plane if there is an accident. A rocket shoots his seat out of the plane. Then his parachute opens.

5 small parachute opens

6 seat falls away on small parachute

7 large parachute opens and pilot lands

4 rocket fires pilot into the air

1 pilot triggers escape mechanism

2 cockpit cover shoots off

3 seat is ejected

Supersonic planes

Planes that fly faster than sound are called supersonic. They are speciallly designed to fly at high speeds. Their wings and bodies are very thin and sharp. Their engines are extremely powerful. Supersonic aircraft are very noisy. As they pass overhead people on the ground hear a bang like thunder.

This MIG fighter has a sharp pointed shape. This helps it fly faster than sound.

This transport plane is not supersonic. Its rounded nose and thick wings slow it down.

Many supersonic planes have wings shaped like a triangle. This is called a delta wing. This French Mirage jet has a delta wing. It can fly very fast indeed.

Concorde and the Space Shuttle

The first supersonic aircraft were powered by rockets. Engineers used these aircraft to learn about flying at high speed. They built fast fighter planes. Then they made plans for a supersonic airliner that could carry passengers. They gave Concorde a narrow delta wing.

Space Shuttle

Concorde flies smoothly at more than twice the speed of sound. It can fly much higher than other airliners. Here you can see how many people are needed at the airport to get Concorde ready for a flight.

The Space Shuttle is a new kind of aircraft. It is part plane and part spacecraft. It is sent into space by a powerful rocket. Then it circles round the earth. The pilot is then able to land it back on earth, like an ordinary glider. Here the Space Shuttle is being carried on the back of a Jumbo Jet.

Helicopters

Helicopters do not need runways. They take off and land vertically. The large rotor on top keeps the helicopter in the air. The small rotor on the tail is used to steer it in the right direction. Helicopters can stay still in the air. This is useful for rescuing people or for delivering heavy loads.

This helicopter is landing on a snowy mountain top in Greenland.

Helicopters are a great help to the army and navy. Large helicopters bring guns and tanks to the army wherever they are needed. They also fly out to naval ships and rescue sailors from wrecked boats.

This is a helicopter crane. It is taking a heavy crate to a building site in the mountains.

Cargo aircraft

Some planes look like ordinary airliners but they do not carry passengers. They carry goods. They are called freight or cargo planes. They have wide doors and can carry crates and containers. Sometimes they carry special loads such as racing cars or zoo animals. Even whales can travel by plane!

This Jumbo freighter has a nose that opens to take in containers. The plane in the top picture has a tail that swings open for loading.

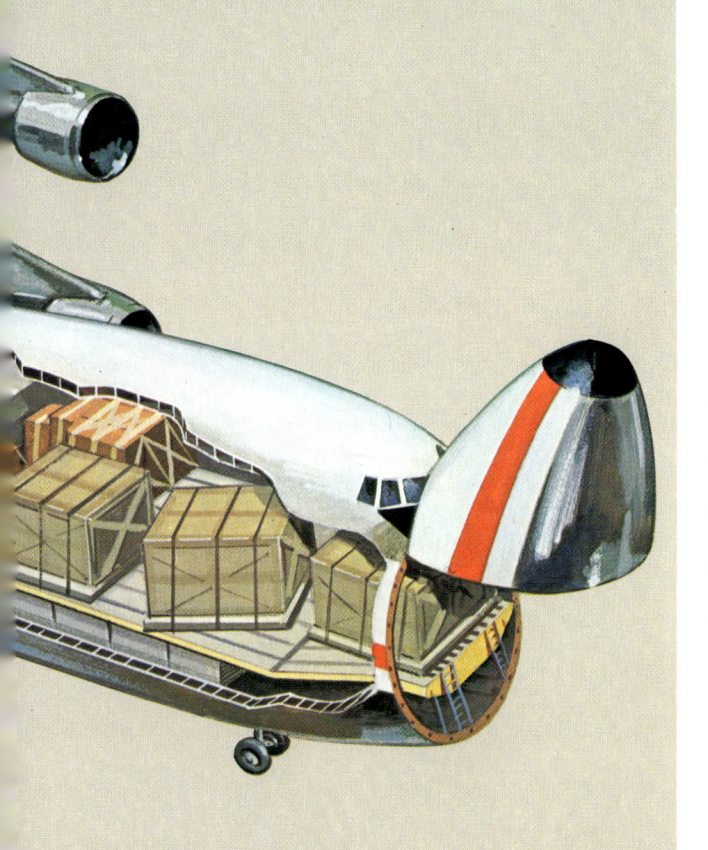

The Super Guppy above and below carries parts of a plane called the Airbus A300. It takes them to the factory where they are put together. It is this odd shape so that it can carry large parts of the Airbus.

Some planes have been made into special car freighters. People going on holiday can take their cars with them. The cars travel in one part of the plane and the passengers sit in another part.

43

Small aircraft

Not all modern planes are big and fast. Here you can see some small modern aircraft. Some look like the early planes but they are safer and more powerful. They have instruments to help them fly at night and in bad weather. Some people have their own planes. They use them for pleasure or business.

This is the Pitts Special biplane. It can do the most amazing aerobatic tricks with a skilled pilot at the controls.

The Cessna factory in America makes more than 8,000 of these small planes every year.

This light plane can land and take off in a very short space. The wings are up above its body.

This executive jet carries ten passengers. It can fly almost as fast as big airliners.

45

Special aircraft

Small planes are very useful. In Australia the Flying Doctor reaches sick people by plane. Other planes spray crops to keep them healthy. People make maps by taking photographs from aircraft. Planes can spray clouds with chemicals to make it rain. These children are having a flying geography lesson.

This Canadian water bomber takes water and drops it on forest fires. Firemen parachute into the forest to help put out the fire.

HOW AIRCRAFT ARE MADE

Here are some of the many inventions used in modern planes. This Harrier can take off and land vertically. Air from the engines is pumped out of nozzles. When the nozzles point downwards the plane rises vertically. When the nozzles are turned backwards the Harrier flies forward like an ordinary plane.

The jet engine is a very important invention. Jet engines suck in air through the intakes. Then the air is mixed with fuel and burned in the engine. This makes a very hot gas. The gas rushing out of the engine pushes the plane forward or upward.

Ailerons are hinged flaps on the wings. The pilot uses them to keep the plane level. The earliest planes did not have ailerons.

The pilot has over 300 controls and indicators to watch when he is flying. All the automatic devices are controlled from the cockpit.

Laser or radar equipment is used to search out targets on the ground or in the sky. Radar signals bounce back off the solid objects.

Early planes kept their wheels down all the time. Modern planes fold their wheels away when they are flying. This helps them fly faster. The wheels are put down again to land.

Making planes

A new aircraft is first designed on paper. Then a model of it is tested in a wind tunnel. Changes are made until the design is exactly right.

Plans are drawn of all the different parts that are needed. Thousands of engineers work to design and build a new plane. It takes them many years.

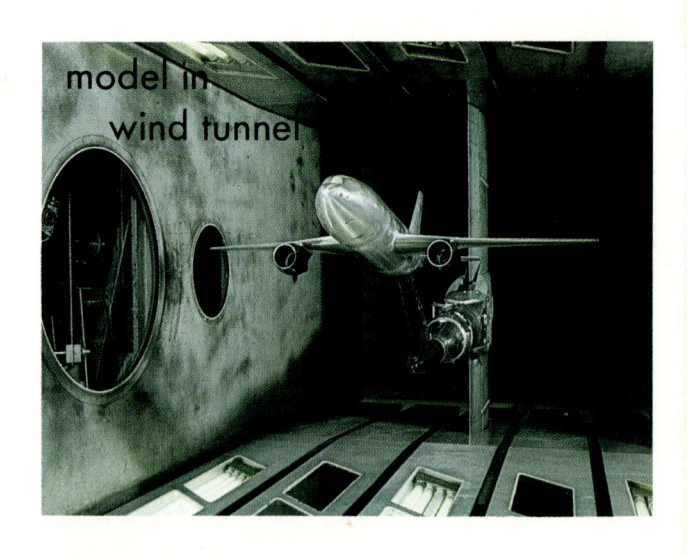

model in wind tunnel

draughtsman drawing aircraft

This is an aircraft factory. Here thousands of parts are put together to make a plane.

Making the Airbus A300

Modern aircraft are very expensive to build. Sometimes different countries work together to make a new plane. A group of six countries are making this Airbus A300. Hundreds of these planes are being made for airlines all over the world.

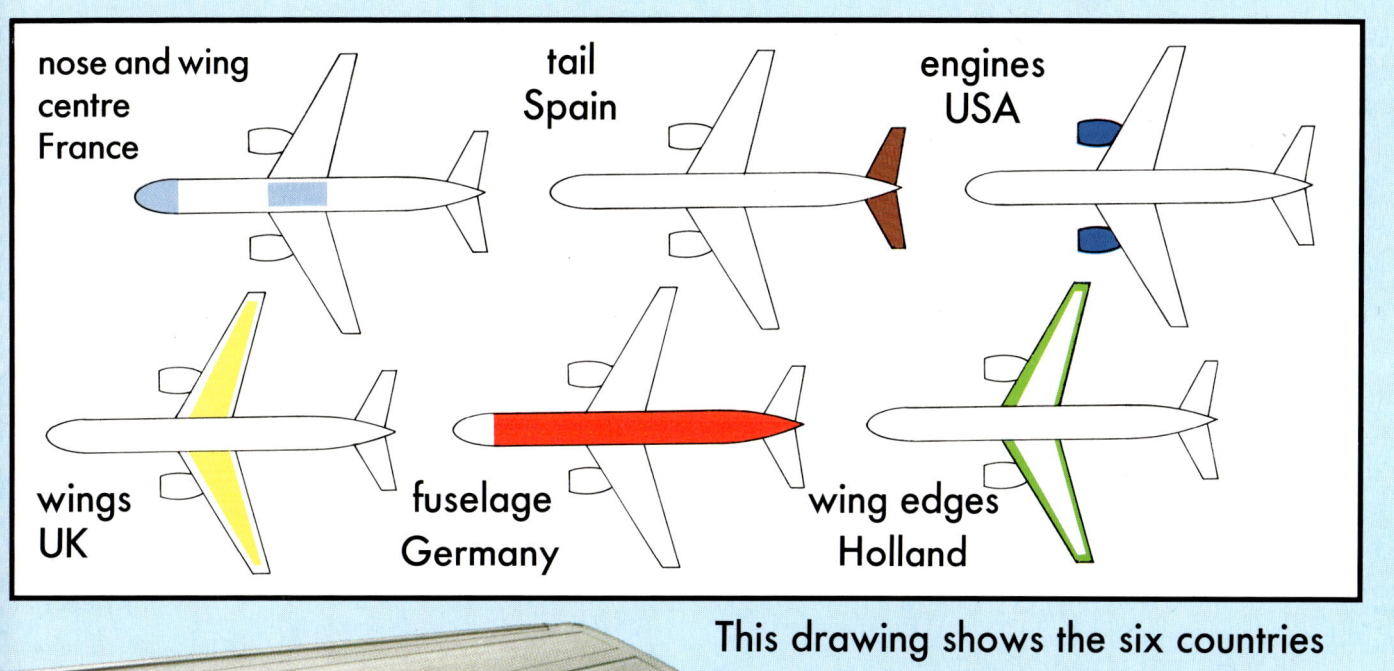

nose and wing centre
France

tail
Spain

engines
USA

wings
UK

fuselage
Germany

wing edges
Holland

This drawing shows the six countries that are making parts for the Airbus A300. A lot of planning was needed to make sure all the parts would fit together. The largest parts are flown to the Airbus factory in France. The Super Guppy carries these parts.

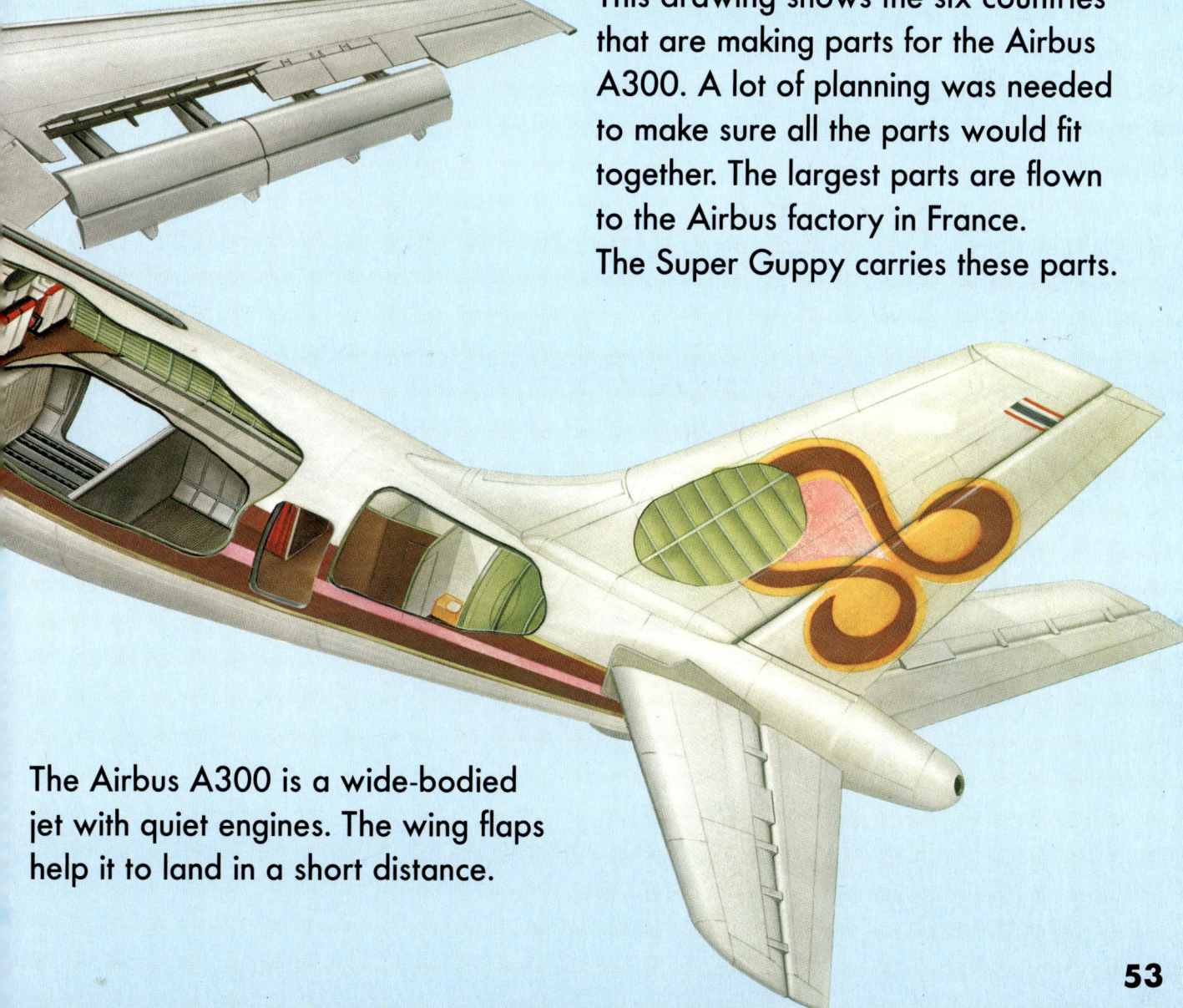

The Airbus A300 is a wide-bodied jet with quiet engines. The wing flaps help it to land in a short distance.

AIRPORTS

Airports are very busy places. The buildings, runways, repair shops and car parks cover a huge area. Each year large airports deal with millions of passengers. At these airports, planes land and take off every few minutes. How many planes can you see in this picture?

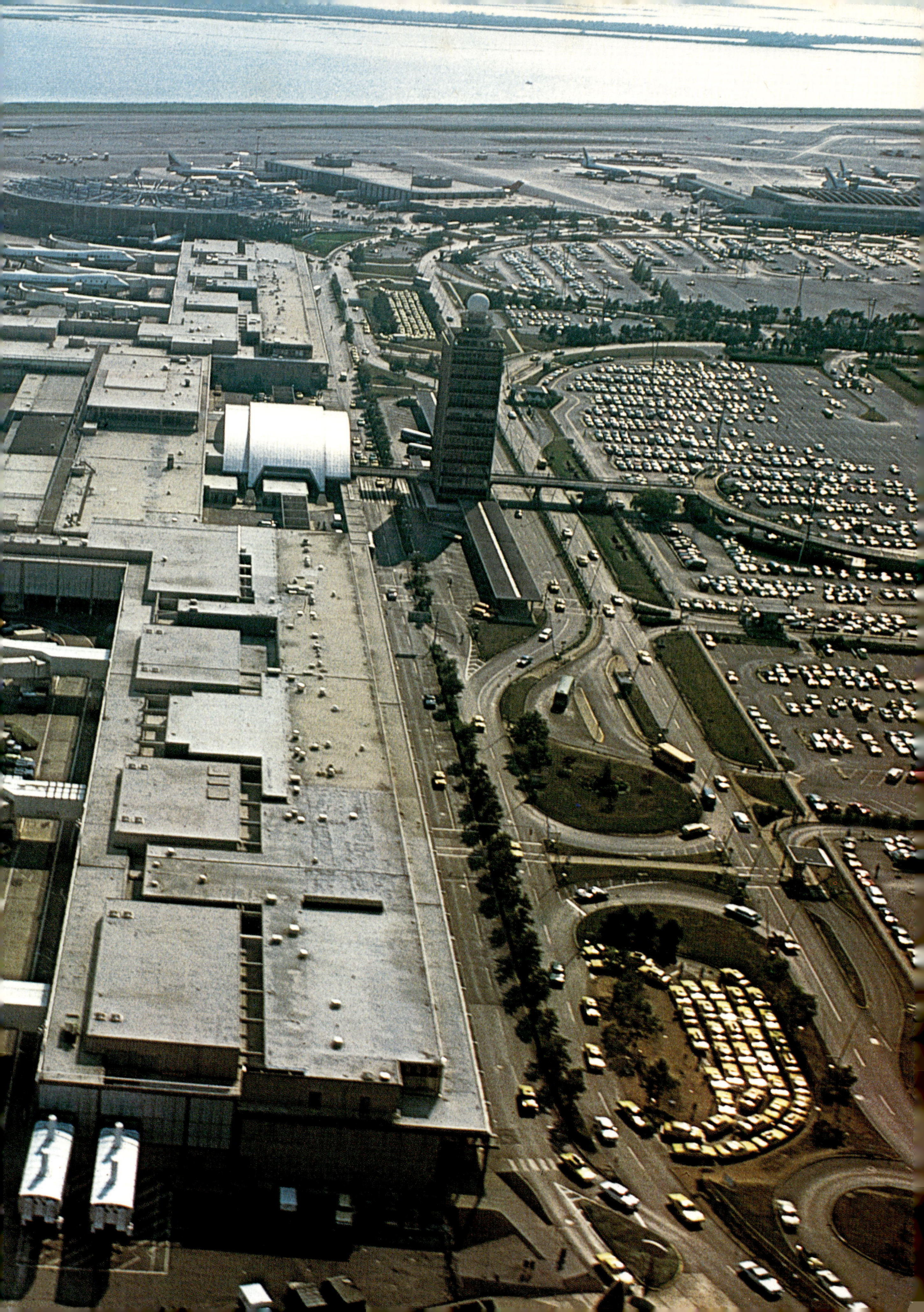

Pilots and crew

This is a drawing of a Boeing 747 Jumbo Jet. It can carry up to 550 passengers. A Jumbo usually has a crew of 17 people. Three of them sit in the cockpit and control the plane. They are the Captain, the First Officer and the Flight Engineer. The rest of the crew are stewards and stewardesses.

The pilot of an airliner is called the Captain. He must fly the plane at the right height and speed.

The Flight Engineer makes sure the plane is working properly. He is often able to fly the plane as well.

The First Officer helps the Captain. He sits on the right-hand side of the cockpit next to the Captain.

The Boeing 747 was the first Jumbo Jet to be built. it can fly more than 15,000 km without stopping to refuel. More than 300 of these planes are now used by airlines.

Stewards help to serve food and drink to the passengers. Stewards and stewardesses work very hard.

Stewardesses look after the passengers. They serve food and drink and make sure everyone is comfortable. They are trained to help in all kinds of emergencies.

policeman
waiter
baggage handler
telephonist
fireman
nurse
ground stewardess
vet
customs officer
engineer
mechanic

58

cook

cleaner

Airport staff

A large team of people is needed to prepare an airliner for a flight. The ground staff work at the airport. Some fill the plane with fuel. Some check that the plane is working properly. Others load the baggage. Some prepare food for the passengers. All these people work to make flying safe and comfortable.

59

Air traffic control

Air traffic controllers tell pilots when to land and take off. They know the position of all planes flying to and from the airport. They use radar to help them. Flight paths are mapped out through the air. Aircraft are guided along the paths by radio. Controllers make sure planes do not crash into each other.

61

Planes of the future

Man's dream of being able to fly has now come true. But people are still trying to make better and faster aircraft. They are experimenting with all kinds of new designs. Some of these designs you can see on this page. Early fliers would be amazed to see how much planes have changed in the last 80 years.

Plans are being drawn up for an even larger version of Concorde. It may look like this.

This new design has wings that are swept forwards instead of backwards. The first plane like this flew in 1984.

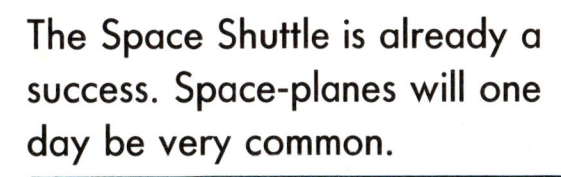

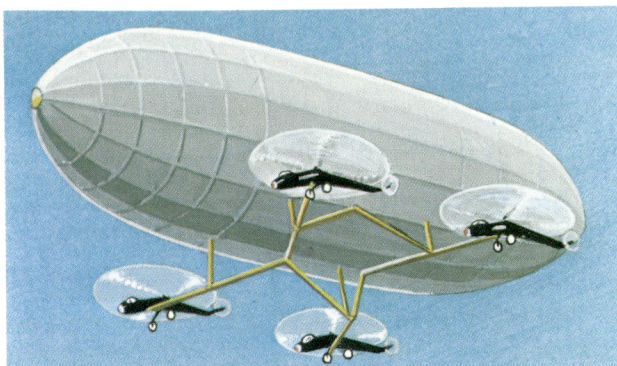

The Space Shuttle is already a success. Space-planes will one day be very common.

This is an odd combination of an airship and a helicopter. Models of it are being tested.

Another idea for the future is this huge wing with engines. It could carry large container lorries.

63

DID YOU KNOW?

In 1783 people who lived in Paris looked up and saw a strange sight. A dog, a duck and a sheep were floating in a balloon. The Montgolfier brothers invented this balloon. They tested it out first with animals. Later people flew in it.

Most aircraft fly very high in the sky. They do not often bump into things. But the Canadian Air Force has lost five planes called Starfighters. They all bumped into birds and crashed.

People cannot fly. They are the wrong shape. If you wanted to fly you would need huge chest muscles. Then you could flap your wings and fly away.

INDEX

Airbus 32, 43, 52-53
Airmail 27
Airports 54-55
Air rescue 40-41
Airships 18-19
Air traffic control 60-61
Amphibian planes 29
Animals 4-11, 64
Balloons 14-15, 64
Biplanes 24-25, 30
Birds 6-7
Boeing 747 32-33
Bombers 24, 34
Cargo aircraft 42-43
Cessna 44-45
Cockpits 56
Comet 31
Concorde 13, 31, 38-39
Crew 56-57
DC 10 32
Designing planes 50
Ejection seat 35
Factories 51
Fighter planes 24-25, 34-35
Flying boats 28-29
Flying doctor 46
Flying machines 12-13, 22
Freight 42-43
Gliders 16-17, 20
Gliding animals 10-11
Ground staff 58-59
Harrier jump jets 48-49

Helicopters 40-41
Hydrogen balloons 14
Insects 8-9
Jet engines 48-49
Jumbo Jets 32-33, 38-39, 57
Kites 13, 20
Making planes 48-53
Maps 46
MIG 36
Mirage 36-37
Monoplanes 30-31
Navy 40
Parachutes 35
Passenger planes 32-33
Pilots 26-27, 56
Planes of the future 62-63
Private planes 44-45
Radar 60-61
Record breakers 26-27
Rockets 38
Seaplanes 28-29
Skytrain 32
Small aircraft 44-45
Space Shuttle 38-39
Special aircraft 46-47
Sporting aircraft 22-23
Stewardesses 57
Super Guppy 43, 53
Supersonic planes 36-39
Tornadoes 34, 36
Triplanes 25
Wind tunnel 50
Wings 6-9